Piet

A streetwise guide

An ABC for parents and children

LUX VERBI.BM

Originally published in Afrikaans under the title *Dwelms – Word straatwys oor dwelms*
Copyright English edition © 2000 Lux Verbi.BM
PO Box 5, Wellington 7654
Al rights reserved

No part of this publication may be reproduced, stored in a retrieval system or transmitted in any form
or by any means without the prior permission in writing of the publisher.

All Biblical texts quoted in this publication are taken from
New International Version
Copyright © 1973, 1978, 1984 by International Bible Society
used by permission of Zondervan Bible Publishers

Layout and typesetting in 12 on 14 pt CgLisbon by The Alpha-Omega Studio, Cape Town
Translated and somewhat expanded by Morné van Rooyen
Printed and bound by
NBD, Drukkery Street,
Goodwood, Western Cape

First English edition, first print 2000

ISBN 0 86997 861 6

Our sincere thanks to **Bennie Klopper** of FOTO STAA, *Paarl*, Western Cape, for producing the photographs published in this book.

Table of contents

Foreword

A

1. What is a drug?	6
2. What is drug dependency?	6
3. Drug dependency syndrome	6
4. What tolerance means	7
5. Classification of drugs	7
6. Categories of drugs	8
7. Ways of administering	9
8. Why do children use drugs?	10
9. From a legal viewpoint	11
10. What happens when a juvenile is arrested?	12
11. What should I do when my child abuses drugs?	13
12. Where does my child get drugs?	13
13. Prevention is better than cure	14
14. What can I do to prevent drug abuse?	16
15. What role has my child's school to play?	17
16. Signs of possible drug abuse	19
17. Where do I go to for help?	20
18. Drugs and crime	21
19. Drugs and Satanism	22
20. Drugs and AIDS	23
21. Drugs and death	23

B

22. Common drugs among children ... 25
    - Cannabis ... 25
    - Mandrax ... 30
    - LSD ... 34
    - Ecstasy ... 38
    - Cocaine ... 43
    - Crack ... 47
    - Heroin ... 50
    - Amphetamine ... 55

23. Inhalants ... 59
24. Appetite suppressants ... 64
25. Other products ... 66
26. Alcohol ... 66

C

27. Encouragement for every reader ... 71

Foreword

There has been a dramatic increase in drug abuse in recent years. Young children are especially vulnerable to drugs because they and their parents are insufficiently informed. Addicts often complain that nobody ever told them the facts. Everybody simply says that drugs are dangerous and that you have to avoid them, but no one ever explains exactly *how* dangerous, *how* intensely enjoyable and *how* unbearably addictive drugs are. And no one ever told them that just about everyone says, "... it will never happen to me," before they start experimenting.

A study undertaken by the psychology department of the University of Cape Town, the Medical Research Council (MRC) and the Western Cape Public Health Programme in 1999 revealed that grade nines spend on average R22 m a year on alcohol, cigarettes, dope (marijuana) and mandrax. The study consisted of 2 779 grade nines in Cape Town schools. According to the study 42% of boys smokes, 50% uses alcohol and 16% smokes dope (marijuana). The same figures for girls were 32%, 32% and 4%. The study showed that addiction to dope (marijuana) almost doubled over the previous seven years. According to the MRC annual report, alcohol is still the most widely used substance, followed by dope (marijuana) and mandrax.

These are only some of the statistics we were confronted by while writing this book. Therefore it is quite clear how important it is for parents and children to read the facts in plain and straightforward language.

This books aims to be your rough guide to drugs. What it is, how it looks, where one gets it, how it affects you and much more. Study it well and learn to face life with open eyes and a streetwise attitude. And if, perhaps, you already find yourself in a situation where drugs are a grim reality, you will discover that this book offers you more than the facts you already have at your fingertips: it is ultimately a great source of hope.

What is a drug?

A drug is any chemical substance, legal or illegal, natural or synthetic, that has a biological effect on the person using it and that leads to physical or psychological addiction.

What is drug dependency?

Drug dependency is when someone develops an uncontrollable urge for a drug and increasingly depends on it to function. Repeated use of this drug limits the person's physical, social and emotional functioning.

Drug dependency syndrome

The process of drug dependency occurs in four stages:

1. Experimentation
This is when the drug is used for the first time to see if it really is like people say it is. This is exactly where people have to decide to say no.

REMEMBER: you only experiment *once*.

2. Occasional users
These persons have moved on from the experimental phase and decided that they like the effect the drug in question has on them. They will join in whenever the opportunity arises to abuse the drug.

3. Regular users
These persons are already at the stage where it is hard to turn back. They will regularly create opportunities to abuse the drug.

4. Dependency
This person is completely dependent on the drug and will do anything to get drugs or the money needed to buy them.

What tolerance means

Your body becomes used to certain drugs and therefore requires larger doses to achieve the same effect. This process could eventually lead to an overdose.

When a person's body becomes accustomed to a certain drug, the switch is often made to a stronger drug to get the same effect or state.

Classification of drugs

The best way to classify drug types is according to their primary effect on the vital functions of the central nervous system, i.e. the brain.

Let's look at the broad categories:

1. Depressants
Drugs that mainly suppress the functions of the central nervous system.

Examples:		
	❋ Alcohol	
	❋ Narcotics	→ Opium
		→ Morphine
		→ Codeine (cough medicine)
		→ Heroin
	❋ Hypnotics	→ Mandrax
		→ Sleeping pills
	❋ Tranquillisers	
	❋ Pain relievers	
	❋ Inhalants	→ Glue
		→ Petrol
		→ Nail polish remover
		→ Thinners

2. Stimulants
Drugs that generally stimulate or arouse the functions of the central nervous system.

Examples:	✺ Amphetamine (speed)
	✺ Appetite suppressants
	✺ Cocaine
	✺ Nicotine
	✺ Caffeine

3. Hallucinogens
Drugs that generally distort the functions of the central nervous system and cause hallucinations.

Examples:	✺ Dope (marijuana)
	✺ LSD

Categories of drugs

Drugs can be divided into five different categories:

1. Socially acceptable drugs
such as ✺ alcohol
✺ tobacco

2. Inhalants
such as ✺ glue
✺ petroleum
✺ thinners

3. Over-the-counter drugs
such as ✺ cough medicine
✺ appetite suppressants
✺ painkillers

4. Prescription drugs
such as ✺ tranquillisers
✺ sleeping pills

5. Illegal drugs
such as
* LSD
* cocaine

7 Ways of administering

Drugs can be administered in various ways:

1. Orally, for example ecstasy

2. Absorption through the mucous membranes
that is
* mouth
* nose
* rectum
* vagina,

for example cocaine.

Dope smoked through a bottleneck.

3. Inhalation, for example dope (marijuana).

4. Injection, for example heroin.

Why do children use drugs?

All children, regardless of race, gender or class, will sooner or later come into contact with drugs.

THE QUESTION IS: Will your child experiment?

Reasons why he or she might experiment:

- A craving for excitement
- Curiosity
- Boredom
- Poverty or wealth
- Peer pressure
- Coercion
- Following the example of a family member, friend or role model
- Upbringing – no specific anti-drug rules, or overly strict
- To improve poor self-image
- Communication problems – cannot discuss things that bother him or her, or communicates better under the influence of some or other substance
- Emotional release
- Poor self-discipline
- Immaturity – cannot make grown-up decisions
- Rebellious behaviour
- Ignorance – unaware that a substance is a drug and/or what the dangers are
- Excessively generous pocket money that leads to temptation
- Friends generally accept drug abuse
- No immediate supervision – nobody to look after the child's welfare, or child suddenly moves out from previous parental supervision, e.g. into a hostel
- Too much self-confidence – "It will never happen to *me* .... "
- Trying to escape to a problem-free world

Michael's story

I've always felt that people don't understand me. I like experimenting and discovering things for myself. I smoked my first joint when I was 12 and suddenly it felt as if I actually belonged somewhere. My friends and I sat in dark rooms for hours, smoking Dope, laughing and talking nonsense. We smoked the stuff through apples, pears and even mud. We also tried out all kinds of pipes. I felt I had finally made friends with whom I could be myself and who didn't treat me like a kid.

One night we went to a club where I bought an Ecstasy tablet. It was great, and all the guys who'd also taken E, were real friendly, like we'd been friends for ages! When the effect had worn off, someone suggested I should take E with Acid (LSD). It's called a Candy-flip. Wow! It was quite rough and I sort of got scared, but it was still nice. Buttons make me sick and I've sometimes lost my consciousness while smoking it, and Coke's too expensive, but I like to play. I really dig drugs. I have to admit that I often steal money from my friends and family for buying drugs. But one thing I know is that I'll never get hooked. That is why I want to try Heroin just once. They say you can get addicted after trying it once only, but it's the coolest rush you can ever imagine.

9 From a legal viewpoint

In South Africa, The Drugs and Drug Smuggling Act, Act No. 140 of 1992 – law divides drugs into three different groups:

1. Dependency-forming substances
such as
- amobarbital
- tilethamine

2. Dangerous dependency-forming substances
such as
- codeine
- coca leaves
- morphine
- opium

3. Undesirable dependency-forming substances
such as
- amphetamine
- dope (marijuana)
- heroin
- LSD (acid)

* mandrax
* metamphetamine

There are also some listed substances that are useful in the production of drugs such as
* ephedrine
* lysergic Acid
* acetone
* ehylene

THE LAW STIPULATES: Nobody may use, have in his or her possession or deal in
* a dependency-forming substance; or
* a dangerous dependency-forming substance or an undesirable dependency-forming substance unless he or she has somehow obtained permission for doing so.

10. What happens when a juvenile is arrested?

In terms of the South African constitution everybody, irrespective of culture, gender, race, organisation, etc. is treated in exactly the same way. Therefore youths are not excused from crime simply because they are juveniles.

They have, however, to be given a chance for rehabilitation after their first offence.

When it becomes clear that youths could benefit from rehabilitation, they will be subjected to a rehabilitation programme and there would be a good chance that the case against them would be dropped.

Young people often don't realise that this only applies to the first offence. Statistics unfortunately also indicate that rehabilitation programmes have a high failure rate. Although these programmes are beneficial in that they protect children against their own immature actions, they also have a downside: drug dealers or smugglers learn that juveniles are not punished for drug abuse. Therefore they recruit children to push or transport drugs on their behalf in exchange for money or free drugs.

However, when the children reach the age of 18 years, they are of no further value to the dealers. Their services are no longer required, and the children are left high and dry with neither drugs nor the income with which to buy them.

At this stage the children are so addicted to drugs that they turn to crime to get drugs or money to buy drugs.

11 What should I do when my child abuses drugs?

* Do not overreact.
* Confront the child in a firm, yet supportive way.
* Show your child the evidence you have.
* Encourage communication – talk about it.
* Consult a professional counsellor.
* DO NOT COMPROMISE ON DRUGS.

REMEMBER: You are the parent, they are the children. Don't allow them to control you.

12 Where does my child get drugs?

It is a sad fact that children normally know where to get hold of drugs or liquor.

Just by moving in those circles, it becomes easy to spot someone who sells liquor or drugs.

A dealer doesn't care whom he sells his drugs to, as long as he gets the money. The worrying thing is that the dealer only wants your money. He never explains how to use the drug or what ingredients it contains. Therefore a dealer could happily sell a child ecstasy that is mixed with rat poison.

Nowadays drugs are so freely available that it can be bought at virtually any venue where children hang out

such as
* night clubs
* bars
* restaurants
* playgrounds
* schools
* house or garage parties
* school dances
* video arcades
* raves
* shebeens.

Drug dealing is, however, done in such a way that ordinary people who do not concern themselves with this sort of thing, would never get wind of it.

Whenever groups of children get together, there is always a couple who are selling drugs or who know where to get some.

The dealers know very well that the children will buy dope from them. They therefore sell it at twice the normal price. And the children pay these prices, because they know that they can get it without any hassles or questions.

RAVES

Since raves are relatively unknown to most parents, I will try to explain:

A rave is an all-night party attended by thousands of people. They are normally held at large venues where deafening, pulsating music is accompanied by gyrating laser light.

The drug ecstasy and raves are synonymous. Many people go to raves to take ecstasy or take ecstasy because they are at a rave.

More or less 70% of ravers use ecstasy and of these users approximately 90% are between the ages of 16 and 24 years.

Ecstasy is, however, not the only drug that is abused at raves. Dope (marijuana), LSD (acid) and cocaine are also taken at these events.

Prevention is better than cure

Since statistics show that there is a definite drug problem amongst South Africa's youth, parents have to start realising that their children will come into contact with drugs and alcohol sooner or later.

But ultimately it is the children who will have to decide whether or not they will do drugs, and what role drugs will play in their lives.

In her autobiography, *Dit klink soos 'n storie* ("It sounds like fiction"), Johanna van Niekerk, a rehabilitated drug addict, gives the following sound advice to parents on how to prepare their children for this decision.

"A child can only reflect on these questions in a rational and objective way if he or she possesses the following:

* Factual information on alcohol and drugs
* The ability to communicate and to express him/herself
* The skills required to make decisions

* A system of values that he or she has internalised and accepted
* A positive self-image based on realistic appreciation of his or her abilities and limitations

Christa's story

I was always opposed to drugs because I heard it's bad for you and can destroy your life. My boyfriend also thought so, but when he left school he went to England for a year to "find himself." When he returned, his views on drugs had radically changed. I was still at school and was very easily influenced, and I would do anything he asked me to do.

My first experience with dope was totally by chance. My boyfriend gave a party and asked me to bake a cake. He gave me all the ingredients to use, including some dope. After I had baked and decorated the cake, I quite innocently ate some of the scraps. It made me feel very weird but wonderful.

A year later, after I had started experimenting with ecstasy, I met a wonderful older guy. He offered me speed and after I had taken it, we sat chatting for hours. I was amazed to find that the drug opened up doorways in my brain and made me feel enthusiastic about things. I experienced an overwhelming sensation of joy en felt I understood what life was all about.

I fell madly in love with the guy and our relationship lasted for two years. We took speed and coke for breakfast, lunch and supper and often at tea time as well. I rarely ate and got more and more dependent. In the beginning it was fun, but I had to keep on taking more just to get the same effect. It made me so hyper that it became almost impossible to get along with me. I was depressed, neurotic, irritated and paranoid. At times, nearly six days would pass during which I would manage to get only three hours sleep.

I could barely do my job and thought nothing of staying away for a month due to "depression." My relationship was breaking up, but I still had sex with the guy because he gave me drugs. Actually I prostituted for drugs.

I increasingly suffered anxiety attacks. I was too afraid to even answer the telephone. I believed the whole world hated me. Eventually I lost my flat and all my friends. I had reached the end of the line and tried to commit suicide.

I believe the most dangerous thing about drug abuse is that the fantastic feeling it gives you totally overshadows the negative aspects. I now realise that for two years I did not grow at all. I never learnt to make difficult decisions and lost all my self-respect.

It has now been a year since I quit drugs. Luckily there is help available for addicts like me. I still get terrible cravings for drugs. I don't long for that life, but I do miss the people and the experiences, the *wonder and ease of a fantasy world that effortlessly transported me away from all my troubles. Yes, I am an addict, because no one can say that it isn't fun using drugs. But because of drugs I now struggle to concentrate, I'm anxious, and I still don't sleep well. I also have other long-term physical, spiritual and financial problems that I never dreamt of having at my age.*

14 What can I do to prevent drug abuse?

It is the duty of every parent to give his or her child advice on drugs and the related dangers. Parents find it very difficult to accept the fact that there are drug problems amongst our youth. Ironically children are aware of the existence of drugs and of what drugs can do to them. They don't, however, realise the dangers caused by drugs.

Here are some tips you might want to follow to prevent your child from becoming an addict:

- Accept the fact that drugs exist and that your child may possibly come into contact with them.
- Learn the facts surrounding drugs and their effects. Be a reliable source of information for your child.
- Make sure that you can spot the signs of drug abuse and be on the lookout for them.
- Make a strong stance against drugs.
- Support your "no drugs" policy with a clear and firm set of rules.
- Exclude corporal punishment as far as possible.
- Encourage constructive communication.
- Respect your child's process of growing up.
- Encourage your child to participate in enjoyable and challenging activities that will keep his or her attention away from drugs.
- Spend more quality time with your child.
- Show your child that you care.
- Try to lead a healthy life and set a good example.
- Do not allow your child to control you.

15 What role has my child's school to play?

Children acquire most of their life skills at school. They play, discuss matters and do things together. It is the place where a story can spread quickly and because the children spend all day in each other's company, it is easy to imitate the attitude or mannerism of a friend or a rebellious child.

I have given many talks at schools and every time I become more aware that our children know more about drugs than they are admitting to. This is not a bad thing, but do they know everything about them or merely what they are and how they allegedly make them feel?

I have also had many requests to solve drug problems in schools. The majority of cases has produced positive results but will the problem end there? I get the impression that schools want to distance them from the problem. They want the problem solved, but it must be kept secret and they are very wary to act firmly against the problem.

Experimentation with drugs has long been a problem in primary schools and the overwhelming majority of children who abuses drugs is still at school. As parents cannot give their children the best education possible in isolation, it is clear and absolutely necessary that schools should assist parents in this regard.

Here are a few suggestions that schools may find helpful:

- Schools should adopt a more rigid stance against drug abuse and should implement it visibly and audibly. Children should be able to see that teachers are opposed to drugs and that they are available to lend support or to give advice.

- School-governing bodies should have a clear anti-drug policy and should act in strict accordance with its guidelines. South Africa's new constitution hampers the application of discipline in schools, but schools still possess certain powers that can be exercised effectively. Making an example of somebody is as effective as ever.

- Teachers should know the signs and symptoms of drug abuse and dependency. They should be able to identify a problem child early on and give him or her the necessary guidance. A teacher should easily be able to spot a child that is changing radically.

Typical signs indicative of drug abuse or dependency:

* School work deteriorate
* Appearance and personal hygiene deteriorate
* Have difficulty concentrating in class
* The child's circle of friends changes drastically or the child associates with a group of children who influences him or her negatively

* Rebellious behaviour in class
* Regular absence
* Weakening discipline
* Unusual remoteness
* Suspect behaviour
* Graffiti in exercise books

These signs could, however, also be mistaken for changes in behaviour due to an unrelated problem. It is therefore important that teachers should receive the necessary training to address the problem in a fitting way, because these signs and symptoms should be noticed and dealt with at an early stage.

Educational programmes and lectures on drugs should regularly be presented at schools. Many options can be followed, including:

* Writing essays on the dangers of drug abuse.
* Organising quizzes on drugs.
* Making posters on drugs. This will encourage the children to research drug abuse. Posters and pamphlets clearly stipulating the dangers of drug and alcohol abuse can be exhibited and distributed at school. The South African Narcotics Bureau, the SAPS or Drugwise are also always available to present lectures at schools on drugs or alcohol.

* Strict supervision should be maintained during social activities, such as breaks, school discos or sporting events. All the instances of drug abuse or dealing that I was involved in, occurred during such social gatherings. The teachers may feel like spies, but most children will welcome their concern and involvement.
* Parent-teacher relations should be improved. During school hours teachers indirectly act as

the childs parent. It is important that teachers communicate with and support one another on a regular basis. This will also make it easier to know when a child has a problem.

The above is merely a framework of possible actions. Schools should use their own initiative and start with relevant education programmes at an early stage.

16 Signs of possible drug abuse

Parents know their children and will easily recognise sudden changes in their child.

General pointers to be on the lookout for include:

* Sudden personality or behavioural change
* Regular change of friends or becoming a loner
* Spending more time with friends than with family
* The adoption of friends' status symbols, e.g. clothing, tattoos, jewels
* Secret phone calls
* Restlessness or insomnia
* Fatigue
* Increasing irritation
* Insistence on more privacy
* Inability to concentrate
* Drowsiness
* Inexplicable mood swings
* Start attending social events such as parties or gigs, or hanging out at video arcades
* Withdrawal from family life
* Loss of self-respect
* Becoming irresponsible
* Decline in academic achievement
* Loss of moral values
* Deteriorating personal hygiene
* Sustained illnesses
* Dishonesty – avoiding eye contact – guilty behaviour
* Selling personal belongings
* Criminal behaviour
* Always having money despite no income
* Change in eating habits
* Weight loss
* Using obscene language
* Avoiding religion
* Talking about suicide, spiritual matters or the devil
* Stealing household articles and money

- Sudden interest in pornography or drug magazines
- Untidiness
- Unnatural craving for sweet things
- Co-ordination problems
- Delayed reaction
- Slurred speech
- Inexplicable anxiety and panic
- Paranoia
- Memory loss
- Disturbed sense of space
- Excessive aggression when using alcohol
- Decline in sex drive
- Unnatural talkativeness
- Sleeping more than usual

- Unnatural energy and stamina
- Inability to reason
- Smell of dope or alcohol on breath, clothes or in room
- Burning incense or candles in room
- Hands stained yellow or brown
- Pupils enlarged or diminished
- Bloodshot eyes
- Increased wearing of sunglasses or usage of eye drops
- Drooping eyelids
- Unnatural hunger or thirst
- Giggling fits

Many of these signs are typical of a child's growing up process and should not be confused with drug abuse. An extreme, though scientific way of determining whether your child is taking drugs is to have a urine test done by a pathologist. Typical dangers and symptoms will be dealt with in greater detail in the individual sections on different drugs.

17 Where do I go to for help?

There comes a time when parents can do nothing more to help their children. Then it is necessary to obtain the help of a professional. The various rehabilitation centres in the country have already helped many addicts along the way to recovery. Former addicts normally run the rehabilitation centres, and the atmosphere of empathy and support leads to excellent results. The addicts learn new coping mechanisms that not only reform their behaviour, but also the activity patterns of the brain. One of these mechanisms is suppressing the addict's pleasure-reward impulse so that he or she starts enjoying the healthy activity just as much as going to the drug dealer.

The following people and organisations will always be prepared to assist you:

* Your local SAPS station
* Your local branch of the SA Narcotics Bureau
* Your GP
* Your pharmacist
* Local Drugwise centre
* Sanca (The South African National Council on Alcohol and Drug Addiction)
  Sanca Head Office
  TEL. (011) 482-1070
* Drug Guidance Centre
  237 Lower Main Road
  Cape Town
  TEL. (021) 447-8026
* William Slater Hospital
  c/o Park and Milner Streets
  Rondebosch
  Cape Town
  TEL. (021) 685-5116

* Ramot Centre
  54 Toner Street
  Parow East
  TEL. (021) 922-2033
* Toevlug Rehabilitation Centre
  40 Noble Street
  Worcester
  TEL. (023) 2-1162
* Helpline
  TEL. (021) 410-3400
* Houghton House Rehabilitation Centre
  TEL. (011) 728-0850
* Aspen Oak
  TEL. (011) 792-7543
* Narcotics Anonymous
  TEL. (011) 440-7073

18 Drugs and crime

Drugs give you an excessive and false self-confidence that could lead to criminal behaviour.

The following crimes are often committed while the perpetrators are under the influence of drugs or alcohol:

* Drunken Driving whether due to alcohol or drugs
* Murder

* Theft
* Child abuse
* Rape

Drug addicts also often resort to the following types of crimes to get hold of drugs or money for drugs:

* Theft
* Burglary
* Stealing

* Fraud
* Prostitution

As you will realise later on when we discuss each drug type in detail, drug abuse isn't a cheap pastime. Many children do not get enough pocket money to sustain the habit, yet juvenile crime is rising dramatically. A study undertaken amongst youth between the ages of 9 and 17 in the Paarl area, Western Cape, shows a 47% increase in crime for the period January to June 1998 compared with the corresponding period in 1997.

19 Drugs and Satanism

Drugs play an important role in Satanism.

Young people are drawn with promises of "free" drugs and they also return easily to Satanism because drugs are freely available in Satanist circles.

Satanism as such is not a crime. The police can only investigate when Satanism is accompanied by crime.

I have handled many cases of this nature only to find that the child was merely trying to satisfy his or her curiosity about Satanism. It is extremely easy to get drawn in by Satanism as soon as you show any interest in it. The best advice I can give parents is to consult your pastor or minister when your child starts showing too much interest in Satanism.

Common satanic signs to watch out for:

(Symbol drawings taken from "*Magte van die duisternis*", Evard Huisamen, Lux Verbi.)

20 Drugs and AIDS

Drug addicts can easily be infected by HIV due to –

- shared needles;
- unsafe sex when under the influence of drugs;
- lacking moral values;
- careless attitude; and
- irresponsible behaviour.

21 Drugs and death

Drugs can lead to death in many different ways – direct or indirect – due to distorted perceptions, hallucinations, depression, false sense of zest for life, bravado or the surfacing of criminal behaviour.

Documented cases include:

- Motor vehicle accidents
- Murder
- Overdosing
- Suicide

- Hallucinations
- Negligent behaviour
- Irresponsible behaviour
- Drowning

22 Common drugs used by children

1. Cannabis
2. Mandrax
3. LSD
4. Ecstasy
5. Cocaine
6. Crack
7. Heroin
8. Amphetamine

HASHISH

Hashish is obtained from the sticky glue and pressed flowers of the *Cannabis Sativa* plant.

This drug is sold in solid pieces that are broken up into smaller bits, and is light brown to black in colour.

Hashish oil is obtained by treating hashish with a solvent. The colour of the oil varies in colour from clear to black.

Hashish is much more concentrated than dope (marijuana) and it is therefore a very powerful drug.

Hashish is taken by mixing it with ordinary tobacco and smoking it. Hashish oil is dropped onto a normal cigarette and smoked in the usual way.

DOPE (marijuana)

Dope consists of the dried leaves and flowers of the *Cannabis Sativa* plant.

Dope leaves and pits

The plant can grow in unfavourable conditions and is therefore cultivated in almost any place. It is the most widely used drug amongst young people.

I believe that dope is the most dangerous drug due to the following reasons:

* It is cheap.
* It is easily obtainable.

* 50% of the community finds it socially acceptable.

It is also a fact that dope is an entry drug that leads to the abuse of other, stronger drugs.

It is interesting to note than reverse tolerance occurs in dope smokers. This means that regular smokers will need increasingly smaller amounts of Dope to get the same intoxicating effect. This can largely be attributed to the fact that the THC (the forbidden ingredient in dope) is absorbed in the fat tissue of the body that occurs mainly in the brain and genitals, and is then slowly released. The body therefore only needs a refill to obtain the desired effect.

One dope cigarette (joint) is equivalent to four ordinary cigarettes. Dope contains 50% more tar than cigarettes.

CANNABIS

Origin:
Natal CANNABIS
The former Transkei
Swaziland
Normally grown in mountainous areas where it is difficult to identify the owner of a particular piece of land

Common names:
Joint - grass - zol - boom - slowboat - pipe - dope - marijuana - hash - poison - weed - ganja – greens

Illegal ingredient:
THC – (C9-delta-tetrahydrocannibol)

Legal status:
Banned

Medical use:
None as yet, but researchers are exploring different possibilities that may lead to a partial legalisation for restricted medical purposes

Cost:
± R1,00 per gram or R50,00 per "banky"

Selling method:
Stop - finger - arm - parcel - section - small plastic bank bag ("banky") – matchbox full - compressed for export purposes

Different ways of packing dope and part of the stem of a dope plant

Photo: SANAB

Methods of usage:

- Smoked in cigarette form (slowboat, joint or zol) or in a broken bottleneck or dope pipe (pipe)
- Dope tea or cookies can also be made from it.
- Because dope does not burn easily, it is usually mixed with a small amount of tobacco – this process is called "salting".

Physical signs:

- Dope smell on breath or on clothes (sweet, heavy smell)
- Presence of broken bottles, pipes, papers used to roll dope in, such as magazine pages, newsprint, telephone directory pages or Rizla papers (joints are rolled with these), torn cigarette boxes and torn pieces of cigarette box lids used as "filters" in joints
- A generally untidy environment (dope makes the user carefree and indifferent to his or her surroundings)
- Eye drops (used frequently while and after smoking a joint to conceal bloodshot eyes
- Incense or air fresheners (dope has a strong smell, but it can be camouflaged by burning incense or spraying air freshener)
- Cigarette roller machines (normally about half the size of a 20-pack of cigarettes, with a plastic sheet rolled over two rollers and a metal base), especially when the suspected user does not roll his or own cigarettes with ordinary tobacco
- Brown or yellow stains on fingers or hands (rare, even in frequent smokers). Best to check the tongue of the user for yellow colouring, except if he or she smokes cigarettes, in which case the tongue will be stained anyway.

Signs of addiction:
- Bloodshot eyes
- Drooping eyelids
- Unnatural thirst or hunger (called "munchies")
- Uncontrollable moods
- Talkativeness
- Impaired judgement
- Giggling fits
- Impaired perception
- Carefree attitude
- Excessive friendliness
- Increased self-confidence

Withdrawal symptoms:
- Restlessness
- Argumentativeness
- Aggression
- Insomnia
- Mood swings and irritability
- Lack of self-control
- Lethargy
- Irritability
- Nausea
- Decrease in appetite
- Headaches
- Irrationality

Dangers:
- Accidents due to distorted perception
- Excessive aggression when taken in conjunction with alcohol
- Anxiety that leads to toxic psychosis
- Physical damage in the form of
    - → bronchial irritation
    - → lung cancer
    - → chromosome damage

→ disruption of the ovulation hormones and cycle
→ sterility
→ disturbance of the body's immune system
→ damage to unborn foetus
→ permanent brain damage

Selma's story

I get stressed very easily. Everything stresses me out and I find it impossible to unwind after a hard day. A friend once suggested I should try smoking a joint when I feel stressed. It works like magic. Dope makes me feel relaxed, peaceful, and I can even laugh about things. It also makes me relax in the company of strangers.

I don't really like smoking dope. It burns my lungs and the smell disgusts me, but I cannot relax without it. It would be impossible for me to go out and be around strangers if I haven't smoked a joint. I would really like to quit, but how would I cope without it?

In the sixties of the last century Mandrax was prescribed as a sleeping pill, but it was banned as an illegal substance in 1977 after it had been discovered that it leads to serious physical and psychological addiction.

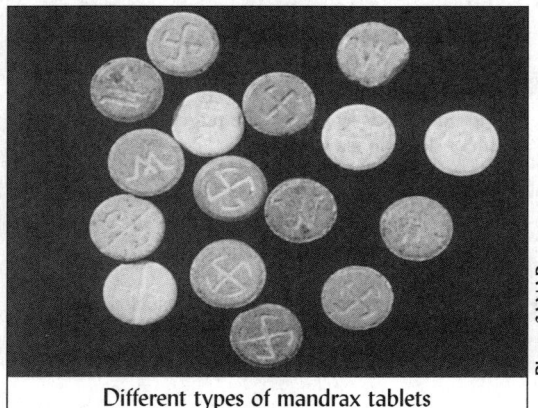

Different types of mandrax tablets

Mandrax is a tablet that is ground, mixed with dope and then smoked.

South Africa is the only country in the world where mandrax is smoked with dope.

A 1993 study found that 80% of the world's Mandrax production is smuggled into South Africa illegally.

Mandrax is currently seen as a somewhat old-fashioned drug and the market is gradually being taken over by crack. It is, however, still very common in remote areas of the countryside where "trendy" drugs (e.g. ecstasy) do not yet enjoy the same popularity as in urban areas.

Origin:
- Mozambique
- India
- Zimbabwe
- Zambia
- Botswana
- Also produced locally in illegal laboratories

Common names:
Buttons - cremora - cream - white pipe. Also known by the motif imprinted on the tablets, e.g. Volkswagen - Germans - flowers - macarena.

Illegal ingredient:
Metacalone

Legal status:
Banned

Medical uses:
Formerly as sleeping pill, none since banned

Cost:
± R35,00 to R50,00 per tablet

Selling method:
- Tablets
- Sometimes already crushed into powder with a joint of dope (known as a "unit")

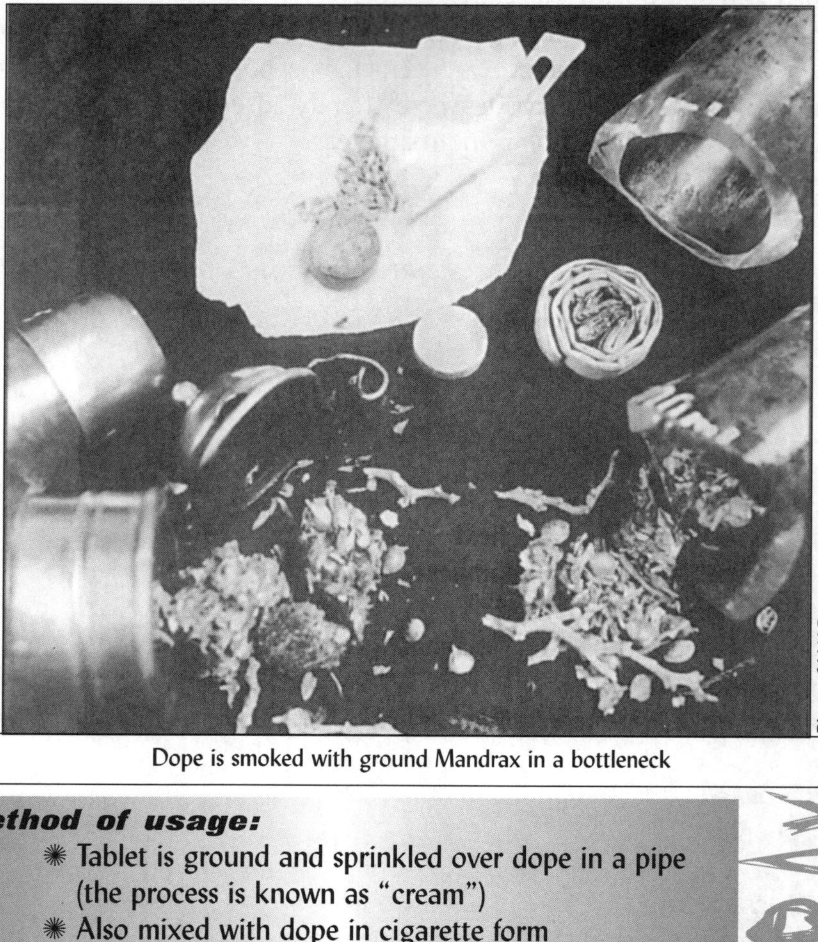

Dope is smoked with ground Mandrax in a bottleneck

Method of usage:
- Tablet is ground and sprinkled over dope in a pipe (the process is known as "cream")
- Also mixed with dope in cigarette form

Physical signs:
- Hands stained yellow
- Presence of bottlenecks, pipes and tin foil in which tablets were wrapped
- As well as all signs applicable to dope

Signs of addiction:
- Drowsiness
- Lack of concentration
- Delayed thoughts
- Dull light-headed feeling
- Poor judgement
- Emotional instability

Withdrawal symptoms:
- Insomnia
- Anxiety
- Nervousness
- Nausea and vomiting
- Stomach aches
- Hallucinations
- Convulsions

Dangers:
- Mental inertia
- Lack of alertness
- Death by overdose
- Collapse of respiratory and blood circulation systems
- Powerful physiological addiction
- Affected spinal marrow
- Weight loss and emaciation

Dave's story

For a while some friends and I smoked dope in the afternoons after school. It was nice, but not as exciting as I thought it would be. Dope also makes me sleepy and foggy. The thought of going into the gangster areas to score buttons provided me with the excitement I needed.

A mandrax rush is amazing! We usually went and sat crouched against a wall with a white pipe. While inhaling the smoke, you slowly get up and keep it inside your lungs for as long as possible. The rush is wicked! It feels like water slowly rising up from your feet to your head. When you exhale, the rush is just as intense so that you slowly sink back into a crouched position. The feeling is overwhelming. But most of the time it also makes me sick so that I have to throw up. Sometimes all the guys around you are vomiting and it's really disgusting to see.

By the time we made it to grade twelve we were a miserable lot. We were scruffy, antisocial and didn't participate in any sports. (I used to be an excellent sportsman.) Some of my buddies failed their final exams. I barely passed but didn't want to do anything when I left school. I just lay watching TV all day and smoked buttons in the evenings. Eventually my folks got fed-up and kicked me out of home. I started living on the streets like a vagrant. I bought mandrax at the harbour and sold it in town at a profit. But because I had become so addicted by then, I gradually started smoking more than I sold. I smoked so much that I didn't eat or drink for days. Within a matter of weeks I had gone from 78 to 47 kg.

A kind Samaritan picked me up from the streets and helped me. I don't know whether I'll ever be able to get my life back together again. I was young and my whole life lay ahead of me. All that's left now is an emaciated shell, a stack of bones incapable of even finding a job.

LSD (or acid as it is more commonly known) is a semi-synthetic hallucinogenic substance, manufactured exclusively in illegal laboratories.

A fungus that infects cereals such as wheat and rye is processed to form LSD. It can also be made from parts of cactus plants or a certain type of mushroom.

LSD is the strongest hallucinatory substance known to man. People who take it usually have bad trips. Many committed suicides due to the terrible hallucinations they experienced. LSD addicts are also inclined to getting flashbacks. They may for example be sitting in church or wherever and get a flashback from a trip they had three weeks before.

LSD is a liquid. Sheets of blotting paper are dipped into it and dried. Then it is sold in units.

The paper is always imprinted with interesting motifs that young people find appealing.

LSD units shown with a South African 10-cent coin

LSD is normally chewed and swallowed or kept under the tongue. Cases have been documented where children placed it under their wristwatches or made a small incision in the skin or scratched off a scab and then placed the LSD unit underneath a plaster over it. Because the piece of paper is so small, it is always difficult to spot.

LSD is normally smuggled into the country in letters or books, making it extremely difficult to confiscate.

Origin:
England
USA
The Netherlands

Common names:
Candy - acid - a - cap - microdots
Also after the motif that appears on it, e.g. Superman - Mickey Mouse - Smiley

Illegal ingredient:
Lysergic acid diethylamide

Legal status:
Banned

Medical uses:
None

Cost:
± R35,00 to R50,00 per unit
It works out much cheaper when split up in quarters so that each child only pays R10,00.

Selling method:
- Per unit – 5 mm x 5 mm
- Ampoule liquid
- Powder
- Tablet
- Microdot

Method of usage:
- Held under tongue
- Chewed or swallowed
- Underneath wristwatch (absorbed by skin)
- On wounds covered by plaster
- Injected

Physical signs:
- Unfamiliar pieces of paper with motifs on
- Syringes and tie-up ropes
- Candles
- Bent spoons
- Injection marks on arms, thighs, feet or any other place on the body

Signs of addiction:
- Emotional instability
- Paranoia
- Strange behaviour
- Hallucinations
- Seeing visions
- Flashbacks of hallucinations
- Disturbed thoughts and mental activity
- Illusions and pseudo-hallucinations (distorted visions)

Withdrawal symptoms:
Not generally known

Dangers:
- Toxic psychic accidents due to distorted perception
- Mental confusion
- Neurological damage
- Depression and paranoia
- Severe anxiety
- Suicide
- Criminal behaviour due to hallucinations

Natasha's story

I see myself as highly intelligent and actually quite conservative. I've experimented a bit with dope, ecstasy and coke, but they don't give me what I'm looking for. I do drugs to get to know myself better.

Acid is fantastic. It makes you feel as if you're soaring. You see colours and patterns, even cartoons. I have written incredible poems and painted stunning pictures while on acid. It makes me feel like Superman. My friend says I once nearly jumped out of the window when I was on acid. All I can remember is that I thought I was a multi-coloured bird high up in the trees of the Amazon forest. Not being able to remember some parts of my trips makes me worry.

When you dance on acid it feels as if you become one with the music and everything is a wonderful, warm, hazy dream. But sometimes you open a doorway in your brain that sends you down a terrible road. Friends' faces turn into those of monsters. The ceiling turns into water and slowly but surely descends on you to drown you. I cannot describe how terrifying it is. Sometimes it's possible to escape and simply shut that door in your brain. After that everything you see is beautiful again, but there was an instance once when I couldn't escape from the monsters. You wish the trip would end so that you could sleep, but the nightmare just carries on and on and on ....

I have taken acid mixed with ecstasy, but it's not strong enough for me. I don't just want to feel good, I also want to hallucinate. I want to explore avenues in my brain that would normally be inaccessible to me.

Yes, I know it's bad for me. I now realise that LSD gives you a glimpse of your personality. You get a glance through the window between your conscious and subconscious. The more LSD you use, the more holes form between your conscious and subconscious. And suddenly it isn't possible to fully distinguish between the two. I've had numerous flashbacks. I am unsure whether I still always know what's real and what's not, even after not having used LSD for weeks. I don't want to turn into one of those acidheads who walk around talking to the birds all day.

ECSTASY

Ecstasy is a designer drug – a term used to describe a synthetic drug.

This term is used for drugs that

* are made from general chemicals;
* are not strictly controlled by law; and

* are marketed under appealing, exotic names.

Ecstasy tablets

Photo: SANAB

A German physician designed ecstasy in 1914 as an appetite suppressant.

It fell into disuse, but reappeared during the sixties and the seventies of the last century. In 1984 ecstasy suddenly made a comeback in nightclubs in the United States, and during 1989 it reached South Africa via London. It was classified as a banned schedule 8 medicine in 1993.

Ecstasy and raves are synonymous. It gives the user lots of energy and stamina and because raves are all-night parties, this drug is taken to stay awake and energetic. It is dangerous because the brain does not get the message that the body is tired and exhausted after an all-night session. The result is overheating of the body, dehydration and an irregular heartbeat that can cause the user to fall into a coma.

Cases are known of people who, after having taken ecstasy for the first time, fell into a coma or died.

Ecstasy should be taken in a specific way, but again the dealer does not bother to explain the do's and dont's to the buyer.

Fortunately no alcohol is taken with ecstasy – only water (to prevent dehydration and quench the user's insatiable thirst) and energy drinks (to further heighten the effect). These drinks contain high amounts of caffeine that contribute to the user's exceptionally high levels of energy.

In the discussion on LSD we learnt that LSD users often experience bad trips, so they take LSD with ecstasy. It prolongs the effect of the ecstasy, while the ecstasy makes the LSD trip more pleasant. Mixing LSD and ecstasy in this way is called a candy flip.

When users of ecstasy have too much energy after a rave and find it difficult to sleep or chill out, they take more ecstasy, but this time mixing it with dope by grinding the tablet, or piece thereof, and smoking it with dope in the normal way. It is also common amongst addicts to just smoke a joint to relax and unwind.

Ecstasy heightens your libido, and as such is also known as the "love drug" or "hug drug". Ironically, one of the proven long-term side effects, that normally only manifests years after the user started using it, is decreased sexual response and even erectile dysfunction. Since ecstasy enhances your sense of touch, ravers like wearing velvety or silky clothes, because it is highly enjoyable to stroke each other's clothes. Unfortunately this drug is still relatively new to South Africa, is seen as hip and trendy, and has the reputation amongst ill-informed people of being more or less harmless and therefore people will experiment with it for many years to come.

Origin:
United States
England
The Netherlands

Common names:
Love drug - hug drug - disco biscuits - scoobie snacks - ecstasy - E
Also known by the motif that is imprinted on it, e.g. Playboy, dove, Popeye, and Batman

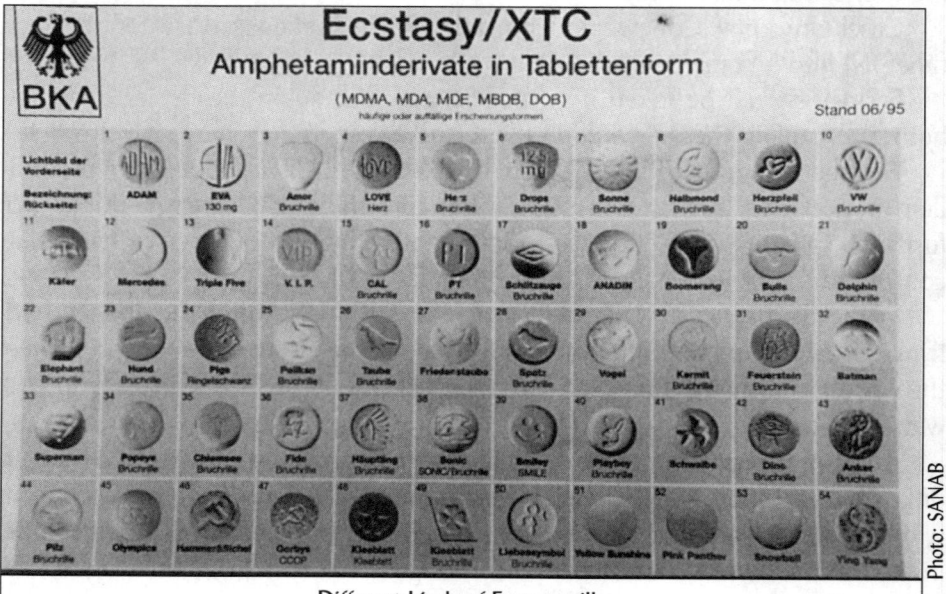

ECSTACY

Different kinds of Ecstasy pills

Illegal ingredient:
MDMA (3,4 methylene dioxy methaphetamine)

Cost:
± R80,00 to R120,00 per tablet

Selling method:
* Tablet form
* Powder form
* Sometimes dissolved in drinks

Method of usage:
* Swallowing
* Sniffing
* Smoking
* Injecting

Signs of addiction:
* Enhanced sense of touch
* Increased energy and stamina
* Enlarged pupils
* Fast pulse
* Locking of jaws
* Gnashing of teeth
* Nervous twitches
* Nausea
* Involuntary movements (mouth, nose or eyes)
* Sweating
* Fainting
* Loss of co-ordination
* Higher blood pressure
* Anxiety
* Restlessness
* Hyperactivity
* Decrease in appetite
* Forgetfulness

- Sharpening of senses
- Dry mouth

Withdrawal symptoms:
- Anxiety
- Panic
- Paranoia
- Depression
- Longing for other drugs
- Sleep disturbances
- Speech difficulties

Dangers:
- American research has shown that Ecstasy causes brain damage after prolonged use
- Deterioration of spinal fluid
- Paralysis
- Physical exhaustion
- Dehydration
- Irregular heartbeat
- Death due to
    - → exhaustion
    - → dehydration
    - → cardiac arrest
    - → thrombosis
    - → stomach ulcers

Clare's story

I had never taken drugs till I heard about ecstasy from my friends. I'm not even the experimental type. But everybody does ecstasy, and it seemed very enjoyable. I also simply couldn't stay awake and dance all night like my friends do. I so wish someone could've told me ecstasy is nice, but that I should never give it a try. Unfortunately no one did.

Ecstasy makes you feel like you are dripping with honey. When you walk, it feels like someone is lifting up your legs and putting them down again for you. Music enhances the effect of ecstasy. It involuntarily makes you move rhythmically to the beat of the music – for hours on end. Before taking ecstasy, I normally only eat light meals the previous couple of days. I take a short nap just before I go to the rave. I normally only leave at about one in the morning. It's quite hard, because my parents mustn't know that I am slipping out of the house. Before I go out, I take a warm bath and dress warmly. And then I take my ecstasy. Sometimes the ecstasy is too strong for me, and then someone just has to hold me till I feel that I'm in control of myself again. It also makes me feel shaky and nauseous, but I dig the loving feeling and the way in which everyone is so friendly towards one another.

I know I'm describing ecstasy like it's the best thing that's ever happened to me. But let me tell you something: ecstasy really scares me. You're never sure of all the stuff that goes into the tablet. I fear that it may have life-long effects on my health. And two days after a rave I always get very depressed and lonely. So every time this happens I promise myself I'll quit. But I know I'm going to lose my friends. I don't want to be lonely!

COCAINE

Cocaine is a white or off-white crystalline powder derived from the South American coca plant. It is the most potent natural stimulant. The leaves of the coca plant have been chewed since ancient times by South American Indians for its pain-relieving and stimulating effects.

It was also a secret ingredient of Coca-Cola till 1903.

Due to its high price, cocaine is seen as a status drug and, unlike heroin addicts, coke addicts prefer the company of people.

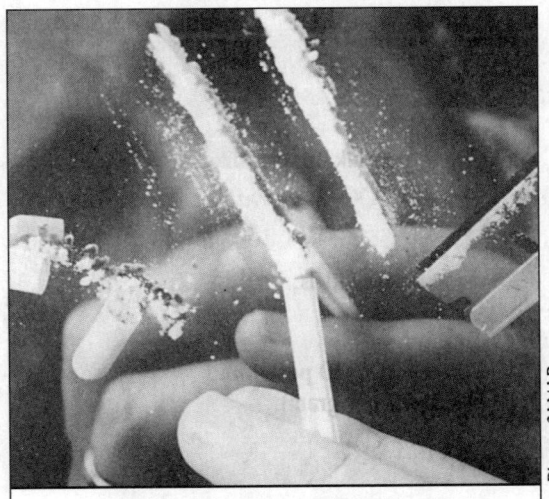

Cocaine powder is snorted up the nose.

Photo: SANAB

The cocaine powder is ground and scraped into lines on a mirror or other smooth surface with a razor blade or bank card. These lines of coke are normally approximately five centimetres long.

The lines are then sniffed up the nose through a small pipe, straw or rolled-up bank note. As I mentioned before, coke is a status drug, and the bank note used is normally of the highest money value.

Coke gives professional people a false sense of confidence and zest for life, and as such it is popular with people who have to work long hours, or who have to debate or speak a lot.

Origin:
South America – Peru
Bolivia – Colombia
Via West Africa.

Common names:
Coke - snow - snort - powder

Illegal ingredient:
Cocaine

Legal status:
Scheduled for use in local anaesthetics

Medical use:
Local anaesthetics

Cost:
± R200,00 to R300,00 per gram
(was ± R450,00 per gram in 1991)

Selling method:
Crystalline powder

Method of usage:
* Sniffed
* Injection
* Absorbed through skin (rectum or vagina)

Physical signs:
- Zest for life
- Excessive self-confidence
- Talkativeness
- Presence of syringes
- Unfamiliar little pieces of paper, plastic bags or containers

Signs of addiction:
- Pale face
- Involuntary movements
- Nervous twitches
- Unnatural excitement
- Lack of appetite
- Sleeplessness
- Fast pulse
- Skin rash
- Behaviour indicative of excessive self-confidence
- Runny nose – sniffing without having a cold
- Bleeding nose
- Constant rubbing of the nose
- Anxiety
- Hallucinations
- Paranoia

Withdrawal symptoms:
- Muscle cramps
- Depression
- Drowsiness
- Listlessness

Dangers:
- High blood pressure
- Damage to nose tissue
- Perforation of the septum in the nose
- Convulsions

COCAINE

- Paralysis of the heart
- Cocaine psychosis
- Death by overdose
- Murderous behaviour
- Collapse of respiratory system

Kenneth's story

My parents move in high circles and often throw parties where all kinds of drugs are used. When I was still at primary school I stole some of their drugs and swallowed anything I could lay my hands on. The most fascinating thing, however, was the whole ritual that goes with sniffing coke. As a young boy I always watched the stunning models and actresses in our home while they were scraping coke into lines with their credit cards and sniffing it through bank notes.

As I grew older, these models and actresses offered me some of their coke, and I didn't hesitate for one moment! Suddenly I understood them so much better. Coke gives you an incredible deal of self-confidence. You feel like you're one hundred percent in control and highly focused. It feels like, for the first time in your life, you're really in control of yourself. Coke, however, made me feel so sober, that I developed a craving for all kinds of other stimulants. I became a heavy smoker and drinker. The problem with coke is that you only feel great for about twenty minutes. After that you need more to recapture that feeling. And coke is very, very expensive. The day after you have used it, you become incredibly irritated and your nose is very sensitive. After having regularly used it for a few months, I had a runny nose all the time, it often bled, and my sinuses were blocked. I also became terribly paranoid and my skin was feeling itchy, almost as if worms were crawling under it.

Fortunately my parents realised something was wrong and could afford to send me to a rehabilitation clinic. I won't touch drugs ever again. Drugs are a lie.

CRACK

Crack is obtained by treating cocaine with chemicals and then boiling it. A crystal is formed that is then smoked. This method is known as "freebasing".

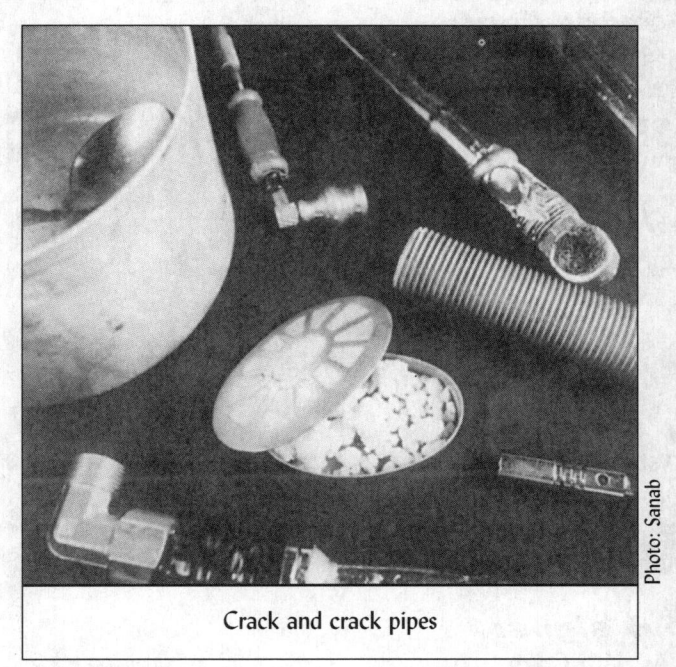

Crack and crack pipes

Photo: Sanab

The name of the drug is derived from the cracking sound the crystal makes when being smoked. Crack is extremely dangerous, because you never know which chemicals were used to produce it. Serious burns have been caused when highly flammable solutions were used.

Crack has a pure coke base that is immediately absorbed. It reaches the brain within four to seven seconds and has an extreme effect.

Producing crack is a very lucrative business if you calculate that a gram of coke costs the dealer R200,00. He makes between six and eight crystals out of this gram, which he then sells at R100,00 each, giving him a profit of R600,00 on a single gram of coke.

Crack is fast taking over the mandrax market and is an acknowledged contributing factor towards community violence.

Origin:
   It is locally produced.

Common names:
   Crack - rock

Illegal ingredient:
   Cocaine

Legal status:
   Banned

Medical uses:
   None

Cost:
   ± R60,00 to R120,00 per crystal

Selling method:
   Crystal form

Method of usage:
   Smoked – neat or with tobacco or dope

Physical signs:
   * As with Coke
   * Presence of weird or unfamiliar pipes

Signs of addiction:
   * As with Coke
   * Anger and fierce aggression

Withdrawal symptoms:
   * As with Coke

Dangers:
   * As with Coke
   * Burns and general damage to body through unknown chemicals

Deidre's story

When you take crack, it's as if you're possessed by the devil. It dragged me so deep down into hell that I doubt whether I'd ever be able to look at my face in the mirror again without being repulsed.

One of my girlfriends took me to a crack house where I tried it for the first time. The rush is immediate and terribly intense. It's fabulous. Suddenly you're wide-awake and really chatty. But after a while you stop talking and all you can think about is getting another draw from the pipe. You get so obsessed that – like me – you'll spend all your money, even the rent, on just one more hit. You feel terrific and know that all's going to be well if you can only get another draw.

When the crack's finished, everyone feels wonderful, but gradually paranoia takes over. I was once convinced that my friend had taken a part of my rock. I felt sure that she was just there to do me in. I also firmly believed that sections of my rock had fallen on the ground. When I got down to look for it, I saw that my friend was also searching down there. Everyone around was doing the same and we greedily stuffed every white fluff or grain of salt in our mouths.

Back home I found it impossible to sleep. I watched the sun rising while I was being consumed by guilt feelings about what I had done and the money I had blown. The only way to fall asleep was by smoking buttons or dope. But still it couldn't silence the voices in my mind or take away the overwhelming feelings of guilt.

I was caught in the grip of crack for a year. After our first experience my friend and I blew all our rent money, and were forced to sell our bodies in order to survive. This in turn made me turn to crack to feel better and to forget.

It was only my faith in God's love and forgiveness that helped me escape from that hell. But my friend is still there. I'm not even sure whether she's still alive ....

HEROIN

Heroin is a semi-synthetic derivative obtained from the opium poppy. Small cuts are made on the seed head to release the white liquid. This liquid hardens within 24 hours into a sticky, brown gum called opium.

Heroin is produced and distributed in different grades of purity, e.g. black tar, brown sugar or white China.

Raw opium and heroin powder

Photo: Sanab

Heroin is highly addictive and has a destructive and long-lasting effect on the addict.

Heroin causes a relaxed and extremely pleasant condition that spreads throughout the body. The condition does, however, not last long and heroin must quickly be taken again to achieve the same effect.

Morphine is an important direct derivative of opium.

Origin:
Southeast Asia – Thailand
Southwest Asia – Pakistan
Denmark
Hong Kong
United States

Common Names:
Black tar - brown sugar - white China - H - mud - smack - mexican - brown - horse - herries

Illegal ingredient:
* Opium
* Heroin

Legal status:
* Banned
* Morphine – schedule 7 medicine

Medical uses:
* Pain relief

Cost:
± R200,00 to R300,00 per gram

Selling method:
* Raw opium – solid form
* Powder form
* Syrup form

Method of usage:
* Injected
* Inhaled
* Sniffed
* Smoked

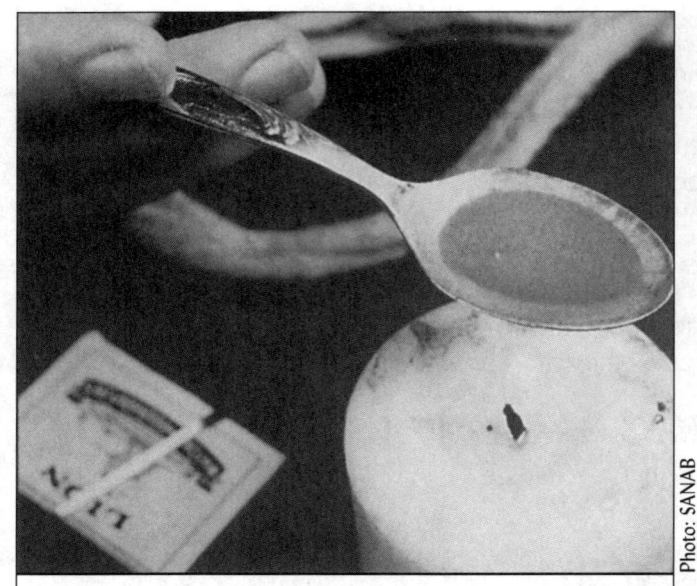

Heroin powder is heated and then injected

Physical signs:
- Presence of bent, blackened spoons
- Syringes and tie-up ropes
- Injection marks on arms or other parts of the body
- Long-sleeved clothing is worn to hide needle marks
- Unfamiliar powders, capsules and syrups

Signs of addiction:
- Small, contracted pupils
- Needle marks or bruises on body
- Sores on body
- Unnatural calmness
- Drowsiness
- Personality changes
- Poor appetite
- Low sex drive

HEROIN

- Constipation
- Slurred speech
- Hindered reflexes
- Introverted, hostile behaviour
- Loss of interest in school, career or relationships
- Reoccurring infections
- Deterioration of health

Withdrawal symptoms:
- Sleeplessness
- Runny nose
- Muscle aches
- Nervousness
- Paranoia
- Anxiety
- Exaggerated pain
- Aggressiveness
- Hot glows and cold shivers
- Severe vomiting
- Abdominal pains
- Nervous twitches and convulsions
- Serious weight loss

Dangers:
- Mental deterioration
- Impotence
- Sterility
- Physical deterioration
- Weight loss
- Convulsions
- Coma or death as a result of overdose
- Powerful physiological addiction
- Sores that become incurable

Incurable sores caused by a needle

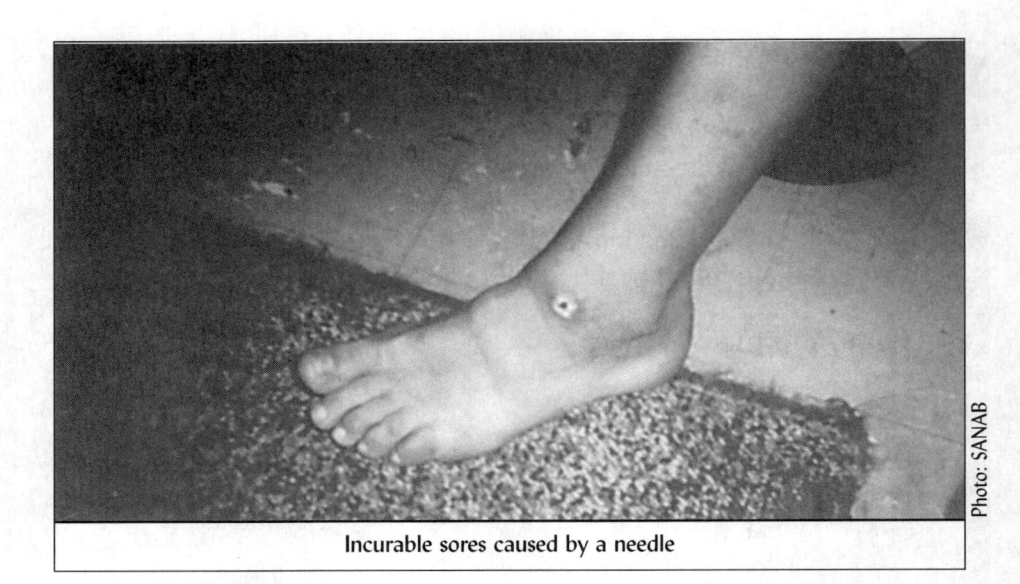

Stephen's story

It has now been eight weeks since I left the rehabilitation centre. At school I experimented with dope, ecstasy, acid and coke, but nothing gave me the rush everyone was talking about. During my first year at varsity a friend introduced me to smack.

When the heroin is injected in your veins, you experience an overwhelming rush in your body and your mind. After that, your body relaxes and you instantly feel totally at peace. It is an amazing experience.

Within a month I became the cliché. I quitted varsity and tried to think about all kinds of way to make money in order to buy smack. Before long I started selling heroin. I got big sores on my arms from all the injections and lost 37 kg.

A friend eventually took me to a rehabilitation centre against my will. The withdrawal symptoms were dreadful. I couldn't sleep for days. I was restless and uncomfortable and had terrible aches. Every muscle in my body hurt, my nose ran all the time and I had cold fever.

Even now, after eight weeks, I still get strong cravings for the rush. I have to keep on reminding myself of how ill I was. I can't imagine not ever using drugs again. I just take every day as it comes.

AMPHETAMINE

Amphetamine is a stimulant that is synthesised in laboratories.

It is highly addictive and also leads to tolerance.

It was marketed during the 1930s as an over-the-counter medicine for a blocked nose. By 1937 it became available in pill form, and was prescribed in cases of narcolepsy and minor brain dysfunction.

During World War II amphetamine was given to soldiers so that they could keep going without thinking about exhaustion or hunger.

Gradually increasing numbers of people started abusing amphetamine. Long-distance truck drivers used it to stay awake, and athletes to improve their performance. It was also used as an appetite suppressant.

Amphetamine gives the user energy and a false sense of zest and confidence. Because you have so much energy, you eventually have to use something just to calm down. Many amphetamine addicts are simultaneously addicted to drugs that give the "opposite" effect, for example sleeping pills.

Amphetamine powder

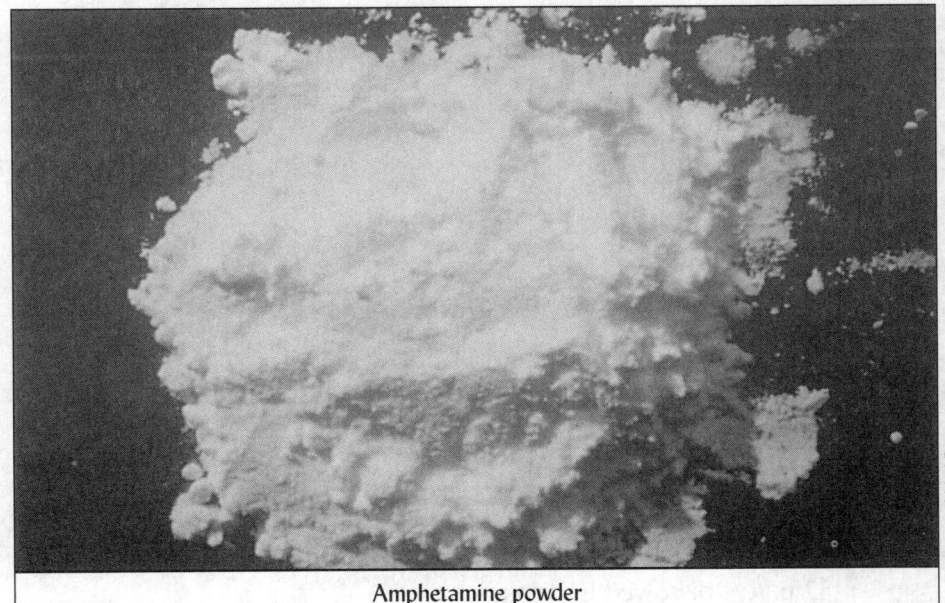

Photo: SANAB

Amphetamine occurs mainly in a white powder form. It is swallowed, sniffed or injected, but can also be smoked as crystallised Metamphetamine referred to as "ice".

Amphetamine is also known as the coke of the poor.

Origin:
USA
Europe, including England

Common names:
Ice - speed - uppers - meth - rock - candy - glass - crank

Illegal ingredient:
Amphetamine
Metamphetamine

Legal status:
Banned

Medical uses:
None anymore

Cost:
± R45,00 to R60,00 or ± R180,00 per gram

Selling method:
* Powder (sealed in tiny straws)
* Pills
* Crystals
* Capsules

Method of usage:
* Sniffed
* Injected
* Drunk – dissolved in drinks
* Smoked

Physical signs:
- Enlarged pupils
- Fast pulse
- Abnormal thirst
- Unnatural energy
- Burns on fingers caused by "Ice" pipe
- Presence of weird and unfamiliar pipes
- Unknown powder or crystals
- Unfamiliar pieces of paper, containers or small plastic bags

Signs of addiction:
- Euphoria
- Irregular heartbeat
- Hyperactivity
- Unnatural sweating
- Abnormal rise and fall in body temperature
- Distorted vision
- Dizziness
- Co-ordination problems
- Fainting fits
- Nervous twitches
- Involuntary movements
- Sleeplessness
- Weight loss
- Dry mouth
- Unnatural excitement
- Argumentativeness
- Aggressive behaviour

Withdrawal symptoms:
- Nausea
- Depression
- Aggression
- Drowsiness
- Listlessness
- Loss of appetite

Dangers:
- Suicidal tendencies
- Excessive confidence that may lead to criminal behaviour
- Convulsions
- Death by overdose
- Damage to organs, especially liver and kidneys
- Paralysis of the heart
- High blood pressure
- Fever
- Apoplexy

James's story

I work as a waiter in a restaurant. Sometimes I work really long hours and then it's difficult to stay friendly and energetic. One evening we had a function again and eventually I was almost dizzy from exhaustion. One of the other waiters called me over and gave me a glass of water with something bitter in it to drink. He told me it would make me feel better and that I would definitely not regret it. I did not think for a moment that he might have been offering me something illegal.

The speed in the drink made me feel wide-awake after about half an hour. My legs, however, started shivering uncontrollably and I gnashed my teeth all the time. I felt increasingly energetic and talked to everyone around me, whether they wanted to listen or not. Later on some people left the restaurant out of sheer irritation, but I felt so good that I didn't care at all.

That night as well as the following day I couldn't sleep at all, and I felt worse and more tired than ever in my life. That evening I was forced to ask my friend for another drink to make it through the shift. This time, however, I had to pay for it. I was shocked to discover that it was speed that I had taken, but was prepared to do anything just to be energetic and awake again. Moreover the speed made me crave for alcohol and cigarettes. Late that night, after the restaurant had closed, my friend and I sat chatting and drinking for hours. After that I drove home totally intoxicated.

For a couple of months I spent a large part of my income on speed, alcohol and cigarettes. I was caught in a vicious cycle, having to take speed in order to get an income, and then in return having to spend much of it on speed.

Fortunately my parents noticed that something was wrong with me, so they forced me to go and stay with my uncle on his farm for a while. I now realise how easy it is to get caught up in the web of drugs. My advice to anyone would be: stay away! It isn't worth it ....

23 Inhalants

There are at least 10 inhalants in every household that could be abused by your child.

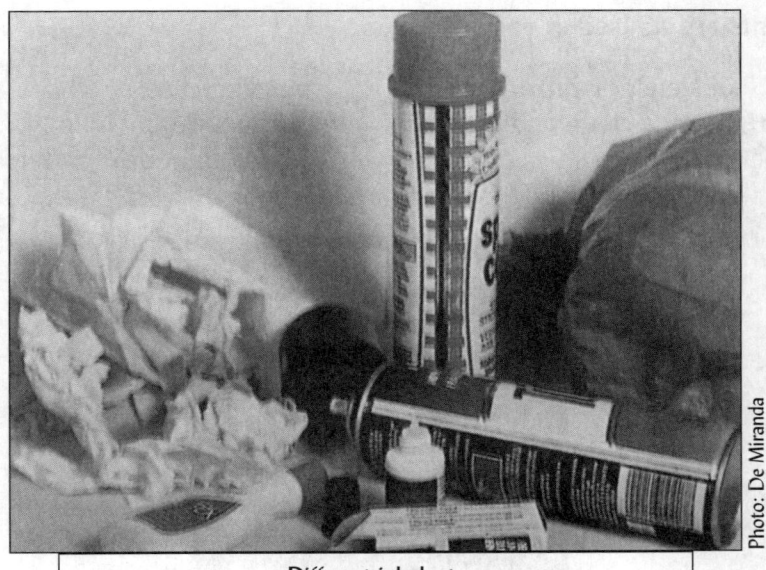

Different inhalants

Children view inhalants as a cheap alternative to drugs and alcohol. The aids required for the misuse of inhalants are also cheap and freely available, for example cloths, cans, plastic bags and handkerchiefs.

The fact that they are so easily obtainable makes the abuse of inhalants a very serious matter. Who will ask any questions when a child buys a can of Spray 'n Cook at a café?

Most people regard inhalants as harmless compared to other drugs. However, inhalants are highly addictive, both physically and psychologically, and long-term abuse can harm the body.

One in three children will experiment with inhalants and the age at which children start using it varies from 6 to 12 years.

Children who abuse inhalants come from all social classes and they normally try it out of curiosity or because of an example set to them.

The abuser experiences a state of dizziness and of a world without cares. As in the case of alcohol, long-term abuse of inhalants may also lead to depression, sleep or even a coma.

The high lasts anything from 15 minutes up to an hour. The inhalants have to be constantly used in order to experience a lasting high.

Inhalants are abused in various ways:

* The substance is sprinkled or poured onto a cloth, handkerchief or clothes and held over the mouth and nose.
* The substance is poured into a can or plastic bottle and held over the mouth.
* The substance is poured into a plastic bag and held over the mouth and nose.

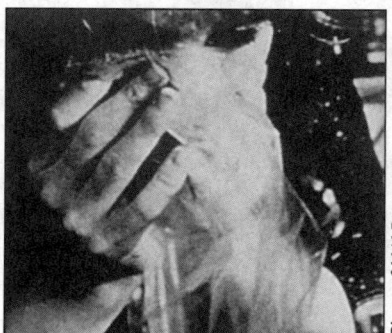

A plastic bag is held in front of the mouth and nose and the contents are inhaled

It is clear that these methods are very dangerous and that a real chance of suffocation exists if the child should pass out.

Children are, however, not the only ones who abuse inhalants. Poppers or amyl nitrate is very popular among adults because it increases the intensity of orgasms and, if inhaled continuously, eases the pain during painful or sadistic intercourse.

Poppers are sold in small bottles under the guise of room fresheners, but is inhaled for a fast and heightened effect. Prices vary substantially between pricey imported and locally manufactured variants, but are around R50,00 for a bottle the size of a man's thumb.

Common names:
- Spray 'n Cook
- Glue
- Petrol
- Nail polish remover
- Thinners
- Tip-ex thinners
- Lighter fluids
- Aerosol sprays
- Turpentine
- Poppers, etc

Illegal ingredient:
- None

Legal status:
- Commercial products
- Poppers – not sold outside sex and specialist shops, as well as private sex clubs

Medical uses:
- None
- Poppers – prescribed as vasodilators (not in South Africa)

Cost:
- As generally known
- Poppers – R30,00 to R80,00 per bottle

Selling method:
- Generally as household product
- Poppers bottles (± 12,5 ml)

Method of usage:
- Sniff
- Inhale

Physical signs:
- Presence of products under suspicious circumstances
- Cloths, empty bottles and cans
- Stains on clothes
- Breath or clothes smell like product
- Appears drunk for short periods
- Deterioration in schoolwork
- Withdrawal from everyday social activities and the family
- Deteriorating hygiene
- Rash or sores around mouth and nose
- Clear fantasies
- Light-headedness
- Drowsiness
- Lameness
- Feeling of weightlessness

Signs of addiction:
- Paleness
- Fatigue
- Forgetfulness
- Shakiness
- Unnatural thirst
- Incapable of logical and clear thoughts
- Irritability
- Paranoia
- Hostility

Withdrawal symptoms:
- Feeling cold
- Hallucinations
- Depression
- Anxiety
- Light-headedness
- Headaches

INHALANTS

- Muscle cramps
- Stomach aches
- Hostile outbursts
- Loss of appetite
- Tiredness
- Nausea
- Nose bleeds

Dangers:
- Damage to central and peripheral nervous system
- Damage to kidneys, liver and lungs
- Damage to mucous membrane of air passage
- Death by suffocation
- Convulsions of the larynx
- Heart seizure
- Brain damage
- Destruction of nervous cells
- Impair balance
- Damage to teeth and gums
- Depression

Peter's story

I went to school in the countryside and would never have dreamt of trying to sniff something like glue or any other household products. Unfortunately many city children also attended our school. These children introduced me to inhalants in grade four. We sprayed or poured anything we could lay our hands on onto our school ties and sniffed it. And it wasn't just a few of us. Often the entire class did it and giggled hysterically. Nobody could concentrate or answer the teacher's questions.

I didn't always dig the light-headed feeling, but thought I was very cool. Before long, I was the leader of the group and all my classmates copied everything I tried out. Even though I later didn't feel like sniffing anymore, I knew my popularity depended on it. Eventually I started sniffing petrol, making me the roughest kid in school. But I was incredibly lonely, and when I failed grade five no one saw me as cool anymore.

My loneliness and craving for popularity caused me to be expelled from school in grade eight for abusing dope. Today I at least have a trade, but I still feel inferior, which often makes me drink too much.

24 Appetite suppressants

Appetite suppressants are mainly used to suppress the appetite in order to lose weight or to control it, but because of the stimulating effect it has on the central nervous system, it is abused and may lead to addiction.

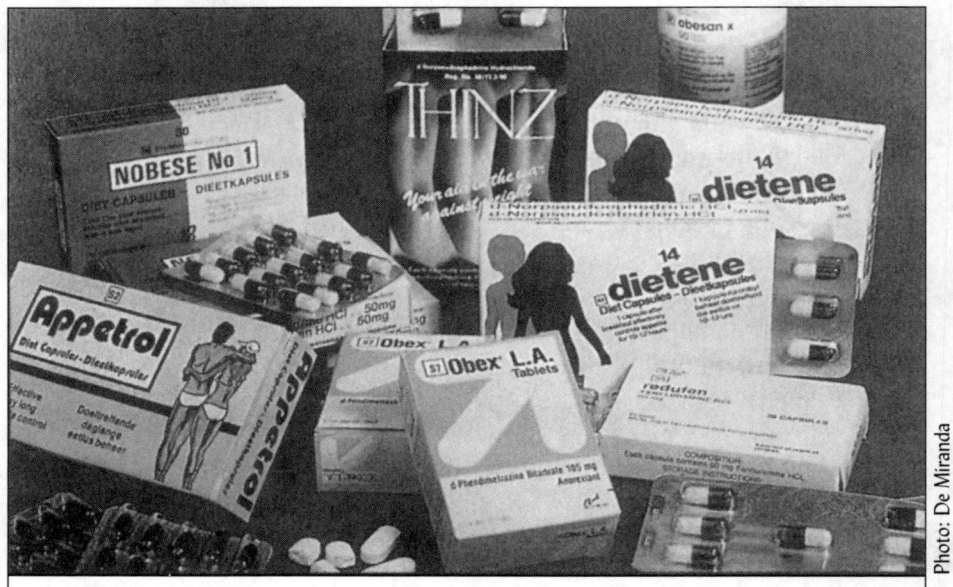

Different kinds of appetite suppressants

Appetite suppressants are very popular with young girls, but boys also abuse it since it has the same effect as amphetamine. It gives you a false sense of zest and confidence, and also keeps you awake.

Because it is so easily obtainable, affordable and legal, young people increasingly abuse it. Abuse of appetite suppressants is very unhealthy and the dangers, signs of addiction and withdrawal symptoms correspond to those of amphetamine.

APPETITE SUPPRESSANTS

Common names:
Thinz - Nobese - Minobese - Redupon - Appetrol - slimming draggies - Tenuate - Obex - slimming mixture, etc.

Illegal ingredient:
None

Legal Status:
* Available over the counter
* Obex – schedule 7 medicine (prescription)
* Tenuate – prescription
* Minobese – schedule 5 medicine (prescription)
* Slimming mixture – available every second week

Medical uses:
* Appetite suppressant to control or lose weight

Cost:
As generally known

Selling method:
As generally known

Method of usage:
* Swallowed
* Sometimes dissolved in drinks
* Sometimes sniffed
* Sometimes injected

Ryan's story

Drugs are expensive, illegal and I'm careful of things I may get addicted to. But sometimes you just want something that gives you a lift and lots of energy. That's why I started using appetite suppressants when I go out to clubs.

A few appetite suppressants make me feel really good. They make me talkative, cheery and energetic.

And they keep me awake at all-night raves. But the side effects are really bad. They make my testicles ache and though I really have a strong urge to urinate, nothing happens. When I eventually manage to urinate, it burns terribly. It worries me, because the suppressants must have a terribly negative effect on my kidneys and general health. The day after I used appetite suppressants, I'm normally depressed and have an upset stomach. Actually I don't even know why I use the stuff, because it makes me feel worse, rather than better.

25 Other products

Generally children are strange beings. They will experiment with anything that can potentially make them feel unnatural. If they like the sensation, they will try it over and over till eventually they are addicted to it. Due to the large number of products generally available, it is almost impossible to prevent abuse of it.

Children are, however, not the only ones who abuse generally available products; anyone can get addicted to anything.

Examples of everyday products are:

- Chocolate
- Coffee
- Tea
- Coca-Cola
- Sleeping pills
- Headache tablets

- Cough medicine
- Tranquillisers
- Cigarettes
- Adrenaline
- Anaesthetics
- Energy drinks, etc.

26 Alcohol

Although socially acceptable and freely available, alcohol is also viewed as a drug.

Acute alcoholic intoxication presents all the symptoms caused by a central nervous system suppressant. Rowdiness and aggression also accompany alcohol abuse.

There is no need for alcohol to be digested. It is absorbed into a person's bloodstream through the stomach. Once there, nothing can be done to prevent the effect. All the drinker can do, is wait for the alcohol to be digested by the liver. The liver takes approximately one and a half hour to digest the alcoholic content of one drink; and this period increases with each drink taken after the first one.

Alcohol as generally known

The sale of liquor to persons under the age of 18 is prohibited. This illegal status of liquor makes it all the more attractive to children and their boozing achievements make them popular amongst their friends. In most cases, however, children are unfortunately simply prohibited from drinking, without being made aware of the dangers of alcohol. They are therefore under the impression that they are not allowed to drink merely because they are not 18 yet.

Despite the fact that liquor may not be sold to teenagers, there are numerous instances when children are exposed to alcohol, for example:

* Children who buy liquor at shebeens.
* They may have a friend who is, or appears to be, 18 and he is appointed to buy liquor for the group.
* Youths are offered liquor by adults who have hidden motives.
* Children steal liquor from parents, family or friends.
* Adequate control is not exercised at bars and night-clubs.
* Youths pretend to be adults.
* Children abuse alcohol with the blessing of parents or guardians.

It is easy to see that there are many ways for children to get hold of alcohol.

Common names:
Juice - dop - booze

Illegal ingredient:
None

Legal status:
Available to persons over the age of 18

Medical uses:
Pure ethyl alcohol – sterilisation of surgical instruments

Cost:
* As is generally known
* However, youths are prepared to pay as much as double the value

Selling method:
As is generally known

Method of usage:
* Drinking
* Sometimes injected

Physical signs:
* Liquor missing from liquor cabinet
* Presence of empty bottles and cans under suspicious circumstances
* Smell of alcohol on breath or clothes
* Obviously under the influence
* Carefree attitude
* Rowdiness
* Aggressive behaviour

Signs of addiction:
- Drowsiness
- Lack of concentration
- Sluggish thoughts
- Impaired social, interpersonal and/or economic functioning
- Loss of co-ordination
- Impaired speech
- Loss of inhibitions
- Use of other drugs
- Sleeping more than usual
- Nausea
- Headaches
- Dry mouth
- Exhaustion
- Unnatural thirst

Withdrawal symptoms:
- Sleeplessness
- Nervousness
- Shivers
- Nervous twitches
- Aggression
- Physical discomfort
- Skin rash

Dangers:
- Mental deterioration
- Lack of watchfulness
- Accidents due to distorted perception
- Damage to organs such as liver and kidneys
- Blackouts
- Convulsions
- Death from overdose
- Powerful physiological addiction
- Destruction of body's natural immune system

GENERAL PROBLEMS SURROUNDING ALCOHOLISM

The drinking of an alcoholic influences his or her friends and family; they are involved in the illness. They feel hurt, guilty and ashamed and adopt the problems of the alcoholic, which makes them equally sick.

Alcohol abuse leads to the break-up of marriages and households. It costs people their jobs, their integrity and their friends. It makes people poor, leads to antisocial behaviour and even criminal records because of irresponsible behaviour. Prolonged alcohol abuse affects your health and eventually causes death.

The papers are full of stories about drunken driving. During September 1999 a girl of 15 from Stellenbosch in the Western Cape died after taking a spin around the block with her 16-year-old friend in his mother's car. He was under the influence of alcohol and did not have a driver's licence.

During the same month a family from Durbanville, also in the Western Cape, was killed in a head-on collision after a drunken driver had passed another car.

In both these cases the drunken drivers survived and now have a criminal record and endless feelings of guilt to deal with.

In a study undertaken by a Cape Town psychologist, the following facts came to light:

* Children as young as 13 and 14 years call Childline enquiring about abortions and AIDS.
* Teenagers prefer strong liquor that they can swallow quickly. If they start drinking at a party at 19:00, they can be as drunk as lords in about an hour and a half, but at 24:00, when their parents come to fetch them, they can be sober again.
* Over the last five years the average age of people admitted to rehabilitation centres for alcohol and drug addiction has been between 14 and 25 years.

27 Encouragement for every reader

You say: "It's impossible!"
God says: Nothing is impossible! (Lk 1:37; 18:27; Gen 18:14).

You say: "I am too tired ..."
God says: I will give you rest (Mt 1:28-30).

You say: "Nobody really cares about me."
God says: I love you (1 Jn 3:1; Jn 13:34).

You say: "I cannot go on ..."
God says: My grace is sufficient for you (2 Cor 12:19).

You say: "I just don't know what to do."
God says: I will make straight all your paths (Prov 3:5-6).

You say: "I cannot do it!"
God says: You can do everything because I give you strength (Phil 4:13).

You say: "I really cannot do it!"
God says: But I can (2 Cor 9:8).

You say: "It isn't worth it."
God says: I work for the good of those who love Me (Rom 8:28).

You say: "I cannot forgive myself."
God says: I forgive you (1 Jn 1:9; Rom 8:1).

You say: "I cannot handle it."
God says: I will supply every need of yours (Phil 4:19).

You say: "I am scared!"
God says: Fear not, for I am with you (Is 41:10).

You say: "But I am still scared ..."
God says: I did not give you a spirit of timidity but a spirit of power ... (2 Tim 1:7).

You say: "I am worried and frustrated most of the time."
God says: Cast all your anxieties on me, for I care about you (I Pet 5:7).

You say: "I don't think I received the ability to believe."
God says: I have assigned a measure of faith to everyone (Rom 12:3).

You say: "I am not intelligent enough."
God says: I made Jesus Christ your wisdom (I Cor 1:30).

You say: "I feel so lonely!"
God says: I will never fail you nor forsake you! (Heb 13:5).

(Source: *Instructions to glory*, quoted from JOY! magazine, June 1999:51.)

Drugs *are* a problem amongst our youth. Fortunately help is available. Never give up hope, talk to the right people and, above all, never stop praying.

I am not saying that a prayer and Bible verse will fix everything, but the Bible tells us that Jesus understands our weaknesses, because He Himself was tempted. He came to earth as a man, and therefore He felt the same emotions, experienced the same fear, and was confronted by the same temptations we have to face.

Jesus is our example of how to lead a good life – a satisfactory life. When our eyes remain on Him, He will show us where to go and what to do. One way of keeping our eyes on Him is by reading the Bible. And when you ask yourself: "What would Jesus do?" you will always find the answer in the Bible.

Keep these verses handy in times when you are looking for answers on life's tricky questions:

I AM SCARED

So do not fear, for I am with you; do not be dismayed, for I am your God. I will strengthen you and help you; I will uphold you with my righteous right hand (Isa 41:10).

Surely God is my salvation; I will trust and not be afraid. The LORD, the LORD, is my strength and my song; he has become my salvation (Isa 12:2).

Be strong and courageous. Do not be afraid or terrified because of them, for the LORD your God goes with you; he will never leave you nor forsake you (Dt 31:6).

I AM WORRIED

Therefore I tell you, do not worry about your life, what you will eat or drink; or about your body, what you will wear. Is not life more important than food, and the body more important than clothes? Look at the birds of the air; they do not sow or reap or store away in barns, and yet your heavenly Father feeds them. Are you not much more valuable than they? (Mt 6:25-26).

And my God will meet all your needs according to his glorious riches in Christ Jesus (Php 4:19).

... your Father knows what you need before you ask him (Mt 6:8).

I AM DEPRESSED

When you pass through the waters, I will be with you; and when you pass through the rivers, they will not sweep over you. When you walk through the fire, you will not be burned; the flames will not set you ablaze (Isa 43:2).

DRUGS AND ALCOHOL

In the day of my trouble I will call to you, for you will answer me (Ps 86:7).

Do not get drunk on wine, which leads to debauchery. Instead be filled with the Spirit (Eph 5:18).

Flee the evil desires of youth, and pursue righteousness, faith, love and peace, along with those who call on the Lord out of a pure heart (2 Tim 2:22).

LONELINESS
The eternal God is your refuge, and underneath are the everlasting arms (Dt 33:27).

Those who know your name will trust in you, for you, LORD, have never forsaken those who seek you (Ps 9:10).

No, in all these things we are more than conquerors through him who loved us. For I am convinced that neither death nor life, neither angels nor demons, neither the present nor the future, nor any powers, neither height nor depth, nor anything else in all creation, will be able to separate us from the love of God that is in Christ Jesus our Lord (Rom 8:37-39).

... God has said, "Never will I leave you; never will I forsake you" (Heb 13:5).

I NEED FAITH
Now faith is being sure of what we hope for and certain of what we do not see (Heb 11:1).

You are all sons of God through faith in Christ Jesus, for all of you who were baptized into Christ have clothed yourselves with Christ (Gal 3:26-27).

And without faith it is impossible to please God, because anyone who comes to him must believe that he exists and that he rewards those who earnestly seek him (Heb 11:6).

PEER PRESSURE
My son, if sinners entice you, do not give in to them (Pr 1:10).

Watch and pray so that you will not fall into temptation. The spirit is willing, but the body is weak (Mt 26:41).

I NEED KNOWLEDGE
... to be made new in the attitude of your minds; and to put on the new self,

created to be like God in true righteousness and holiness (Eph 4:23-24).

I NEED STRENGTH

Look to the LORD and his strength; seek his face alwaus. Remember the wonders he has done, his miracles, and the judgments he pronounced .... (I Ch 16:11-12).

My flesh and my heart may fail, but God is the strength of my heart and my portion forever (Ps 73:26).

Trust in the LORD forever, for the LORD, the LORD, is the Rock eternal (Isa 26:4).

I NEED GUIDANCE

... being confident of this , that he who began a good work in you will carry it on to completion until the day of Christ Jesus (Php 1:6).

I AM DISCOURAGED

No, in all these things we are more than conquerors through him who loved us (Rom 8:37).

But as for you, be strong and do not give up, for your work will be rewarded (2 Ch 15:7).

Surely the arm of the LORD is not too short to save, nor his ear too dull to hear (Isa 59:1).

I NEED COMFORT

Even though I walk through the valley of the shadow of death, I will fear no evil; for you are with me; your rod and your staff, they comfort me (Ps 23:4).

I DOUBT GOD'S EXISTENCE

Know therefore that the LORD your God is God, he is the faithful God, keeping his covenant of love to a thousand generations of those who love him and keep his commands (Dt 7:9).

I NEED WISDOM

... in whom are hidden all the treasures of wisdom and knowledge (Col 2:3).

If any of you lacks wisdom, he should ask God, who gives generously to all without finding fault, and it will be given to him (Jas 1:5).

Who is wise and understanding among you? Let him show it by his good life, by deeds done in the humility that comes from wisdom (Jas 3:13).

Sources

1. De Miranda, Dr S.: *Dwelms en dwelmmisbruik in Suider-Afrika*. J.L. van Schaik: 1987.

2. Van Niekerk, Johanna: *Dit klink soos 'n storie*. Barak: 1988.

3. Republiek van Suid-Afrika: Wet op Dwelmmiddels en Dwelmsmokkelary: Wet 140 van 1992.